SEALED SECRETS

MAGIXIE

Made with ♥ on the Notion Press Platform
www.notionpress.com

SEALED SECRETS

Contents

Contents

Contents

Foreword

Poetry is a form of art that dances with the words.

Chapter1

We call ourselves humans,
but now we call ourselves AI's.
We call this plane,
but now space ship is the plane.
We call this Planet,
but now we call this a Country.
We call them Animals,
but now we call them Robots.
once we call it a Universe,
but now we call it a planet.
- - Magixie
Future and past
past and present
present and future

Chapter2

Is there something new?
a million fake hearts
or a blank heart?
Is there something new?
a nature of cruelty
or a nature of pity?
Is there something new?
a wish of wants
or a wish of needs?
is there something new?
a fake smile on face
or a loud cry face?
is there anything new?
in this cruel world
I wish to live in a place
where humans are invisible
and finally, there is something new.
I found something new
something you've known
It's my own fantasy world
you've never seen
you've never heard

something new to you
someone new to me
there is something Magical.
-Magixie

Chapter3

can you hear me?
can you see me ?
Am I invisible in your eyes?
please find me in your eyes
Am I invisible in my own world?
I want you to find me in my own world
Am I unhearable in this world?
I want to explore me
I want to explore you
I want to explore this world
please find me...
-Magixie

Chapter4

52 Hertz whale so lonely
I want to be that whale
I don't want to be in this world.
This world to hates me
please I want to be you
and give you a little happiness
-Magixie

Chapter5

How big is the universe?
Is it deeper than the ocean?
Am I capable
to see the universe?
is it a universe
or is it an ocean?
is it a universe
or a world of stars, moons, planets?
it's so beautiful
It's an elysian vision
I Just want to cleave to it
I Just don't know why
I am happier to be
a part of this universe
I am happier to be
with my family
in this universe
with these stars, moons, planets...
the universe still goes on forever...
- Magixie

Chapter6

I want my protector
to save me
please come and save me
What are you upto?
Are you there for me?
Are you there to protect me?
I wish a soul
to heal me
I want a soul
to protect me
then I found
there was a soul
to protect me
from you
to protect me
from you
I found a soul
to take me
to my destiny
- Magixie

Chapter7

I am all alone
even I talk
no one can hear me
no one can listen to me
alone soul
even in the heaven
may be
someone can find me
on the earth or
even in the heaven
there is a little hope
that made me
wait for you
How to long it has been?
How long should I wait
find me nowhere
please find me
bring the light
into my darkness
that made me
wait for you
I'm still waiting for you....!!!!!

-Magixie

Chapter8

She is silent
like the sea
deep in the sea
She could express
her feels
but no one
notices it
she is silent
like the sea
she is afraid
of be expressed
to the world
she is hideous
like the dark
she hoped to
be the light
she wants to
be herself
but it feels
so alienated
She wants to
be the best

but no one cares
It's hard to survive
no one can find her
in the deep
the one who
meets her soul
heals her soul.
- Magixie

Chapter9

Hiding the wounds
to heal my soul
to gain my love
I'm so hurt
deep down
I can't hold it anymore
but I want to hold it
until my soul dies
It formed lakes in the heart
it turned into rivers
and it formed an ocean
in my heart
I submerged myself
into the ocean
I can't take anymore
save me from myself..
-As it continues it gets deeper in the ocean...
- Magixie

Chapter10

confused with the feelings
of heart and brain
each depends on another
Just to see
a mixture of emotions
in one face
one in the heart
other in the brain
cause cry and laugh.
It's an evil emotion
save from the brain
help my heart
Rip the connection
Where the true emotion
comes from?
one says
the sweet truth
the other object
the bitter truth
what is it about?
- Magixie

Chapter11

Heart sank in sorrow
building a mountain
in the blue eyes
of the black holes
look at the world
How beautiful it is
don't look deep
may be the bright
will look into you
wait for the time
it will let you
break through it
-Magixie

Chapter12

The cheerful eyes
holds the dakest memories
the happiest smiles
holds the deepest pain
the sweetest lies
holds the bitter truths
Gaining my worth
holding a grudge
the coolest personalities
have much more pressure
they are the saddest
on a side of pictures
they are the happiest
move on from the past
past is related to future
-Magixie

Chapter13

The whale goes along
the blue ocean
The blue sky blooms
in every season
The rain Shadow
of the heart
makes monsoon
fragrance of the flowers
makes the Spring
holidays of the school
makes the summer
fall of leaves
blooms in Autumn
goes along with the world
-Magixie

Chapter14

Like an Angel
in the sky
Ocean of the blue
dancing in the sea
everything is blue
reaches to the blue
in the deep dark
all is black
seems to be beautiful
turns to be painful
everyday everynight
but still shines
all the way.
- Magixie

Chapter15

Falling a part
to be the one
for the happiest moments
gaining the pain
we both are in
different worlds
the path divides
we fall a part
bout souls never
fall a part
waiting for you
my soul dies
hopelessly...
- Magixie

Chapter16

Everything fades away
everything blooms again
but some can
never be replaced
it's too late
to bloom again
sometimes it's better
to be invisible
-Magixie

Chapter17

deep in the dark
shadows of the forest
cover of the evergreen
fragrance of the mud
blooming of the flowers
sound of the chirping
Roars of the wild
dance of the peacock
Jumping of the monkeys
caves of the king
Holes of the insects
Nests of the bird
behind all of these
many secrets are Still hidden.
sometimes hidden things are to be hidden forever is the best thing.
-Magixie

Chapter18

All along the way
the hardships gone too far
The happiest moments
became memories
the saddest past became the dark future
feels so insecure
wants to be independent
can't be dependent
fight the present.
-Magixie

Chapter19

In the dark echo
travels the spirit
A soul with scars
found unconscious
the soul meets
deep Hazel brown eyes
the spirit found it's soul
-Magixie

Chapter20

Lonely wolf
searching for the right
the moon sends the
right wolf to the Lonely
fills it's light
-Magixie

Chapter21

magical blue eyes
searching for something
waiting for the red
feels only the pain
a real blooms
in the full moon
the blue met red
found the mate
blessed by the moon
found it's joy
- Magixie

Chapter22

locked the doors
of my heart
submerged myself
in the deep ocean
filled with sorrow
it's really scary
in the dark
filled with blood
a tiny butterfly
with a little hope
waiting for light
-Magixie

Chapter23

In the Darker shades
I feel you fade.
as you shine bright,
I will get you right.
in the shade of the moon
We rest under the hill.
even when you reach out,
I will be out of sight.
As it gets colder
the memories feel warmer.
even in the dark
I tend to feel the light.
from the soul of your sacrifice
It's very beautiful on a full moon night.
As it gets colder. It gets enchanted......
-Magixie

Chapter24

Snowing in the dark
Raining in the snow
Snowflake touches the ground.
Winter falls in every year
First fall of winter
Our wishes come true.
-Magixie

Chapter25

Grazing at the Stars
hoping for a better world
being a cosmogyral
let it be in tacenda
there is a lacuna
it's an enchanted place
as it never be in
let it into you
follow your passion,
being an astrophile.
-Magixie

Chapter26

Hope is living
in the dark;
dark is in
the light;
light is in
the day.
you've got
dreams to chase
dream high
in your thoughts
- Magixie

Chapter27

Dream about
something magical
your imagination
goes beyond
the world
as it ever
happened to you
your dream is
hard to catch
unique to dream
like you.....
-Magixie

Chapter28

Woods are dark
in the deep
surrounded by the beings
full of arts
never thought
It could feel
so lonely
the beings
Who can fill the light
But It never felt
so bright
the people Who can
spread the warmth
but it's freezing here
full of happiness
all I have felt
being alone
in the dark woods
- Magixie

Chapter29

still follows
the dark saga
following through
my dark Shadows
summoned by evil
in my deepest thoughts
as it renders over
my past flaws
the soft changes
into heart
It Is strange
as hell but
it is unique
as heaven
- Magixie

Chapter30

Wind Shines
in the dark sea
Suns rays shine
through the wind
whispers of
the unknown
will never
leave you
In this
giant world
where all
of my dreams
were built
-Magixie

Chapter31

Beauty in the night

wakes the light

evergreen forest

scent of trees

twinkling stars

blessing the

pair or spirits

that protect the forest

- Magixie

Chapter32

The world full of colours
in the bright light.
one day faces the dark
afraid in the night
goes through the pain
of the curse, hate
you built towards it
it gets hard to breath.
when it's easy to survive
it's the call of the day
to get you even more darker
It's easy to breathe
Just for the kind
- Magixie

Chapter33

The bright face
has much to say
choose to be calm
has lot to retake
choose not to
The hardships
had taught them
so much more
-Magixie

Chapter34

I can feel
the soul of the fear
pierces through me
I can feel it
as it takes over me
It's getting dark
even when the
dark hides
In the shadow
of the fear
-Magixie

Chapter35

Looking at the moon.
in the dark sky
fading with clouds
covered with the dark
blooms with the bright
illuminate the gloom
twinkling in the night sky
counting on the constellations.
aiming at the stars
filled with it's glow
shining through my eyes
on a full-moon day
gold shines from the
heart of a selenophile.
only a selenophile can feel the elysian feeling
in these lines
- Magixie

Chapter36

looking at the moon
I have found you
in my heart
may be I Just
gone through your eyes
may be I Just
felt your heart
in the moonlight
of my darkness
you are the
brightest soul in my galaxy...
may be when I found you
- Magixie

Chapter37

I was an outcast
he was a king
I was just a bait
his eyes are still
can the pain bear?
my scars in his soul
through the dark
he was lost
When I was a vain
his soul pierces through me
I was just a pain
in his prison
He was the lord
in my void world
He was just a soul
who embraces an outcast
he was a star
I was Just a scar
in his world
He meant was
my only world in life
- Magixie

Chapter38

There are centuries
When I need them
There are decades
When I never wanted
There is nothing
When I see through the glass
There is magic
When I pierce my soul
There is darkness
When my soul fades away
There are sparkles
when my soul rages
There is rain
When I need to be embraced
There is evil
which made me strong
There is good
which turns me into a pure soul
There is something
which wakes the witch in me
Description of Humane....
- Magixie

Chapter39

I want to meet you
under the same Sky
gazing at the same stars
have been through a lot
smiles awaken by the moonlight
It was always you
and was forever me
~An extract from Margixie's Journal
- Magixie

Chapter40

In the era of shadow,
I assembled the hitch of my breath
dark yet beautiful in the wilderness,
painful yet thoughtful as soul fades away,
beauty be the dark as it fades away.
blooms as the rainbow in the sky.
reckless beasts hunting down,
the wilderness of the beauty
as it evolves in the dark era.
beauty hides the pain
beneath the ocean of sorrows
it fades away...
- Magixie

Chapter41

I'd love to watch you leave
but I just can't as it sets
magically embedded into the sky
profoundly breathtaking as you stare
you gleam in the brightness of my soul
as it sticks to the shades of blue.
it's a bliss to see you fade away
it's a spell to let you away
As you flawlessly pierces my glory...
-Magixie

Chapter42

As the time pass by
you bloomed as the cherry blossom
little did you know that
a soul is waiting for you
little did I know that
a soul cares for me
little did we know that
we are bound together
as the time pass by
it was casting a beautiful Spell
a beautiful curse called love
As the time pass by
I realised it was a dream
that was never meant to be awaken
As the time pass by
I got to know that
It was me all the time
All alone, eyes searching for you
in every corner of the world. I can see
A beautiful curse and a beautiful spell.
- An extract from Magixie's Journal
- Magixie

Chapter43

As it echoes through my spine
it renders all the way my mind
As it deepens the wounds
If I was a star that died
As it was drowning me
in the unknown world
As it evolves from the melodrama
is cuts me in the throat that surrenders
As if I was fond of its madness
it meets me through just to avert my gaze
drowns me so deep as the mermaid couldn't breathe
As the hitch of breath cuts the ocean.
-Magixie

Chapter44

I heard you
wishpering to the moon
I saw you
staring at the sun
I talked about you
to the Stars
I saw your
tears shredding
under the moonlight
I called you
as my heart ached through
As you turned into a stone
My world blacked out
As my love for you
turned into pain
as it renders as
my anger
as it echoes
into Hate
-Magixie

Chapter45

Darling I Just heard you
in your embrace I felt you
As if moon shines in your eyes
sun glows through your smile
I see the dreams that held you
As if the waves shatter in your tears
I felt the breeze that held you back
As if the sky of your thoughts of mine
I felt the ocean that's holding me back
we're drowning in our dreams...
-Magixie

Chapter46

I got lost
in the world of your fear
trembling in the shadows
I'm scared of my potential
it terrifies the darkest wounds
as they are hidden underneath
It soaks me in your eyes
Amused by the thoughts of mine...!!!
-Magixie

Chapter47

I wanna hear your anger
until It slits my throat
I wanna hear your agony
until my tears end their way
I wanna see you smile
until my eyes get blind
I wanna see you happy
until my Sorrow cuts the way
I wanna get through this
with you...
-Magixie

Chapter48

Minute by minute
As the petals fall
day by day
the Autumn arrives
you know when
Sakura blooms
spring arrives
it fades away
without the clock ticks...
- An extract from Magixie's journal
- Magixie

Chapter49

Trillions of broken million pieces
billions of tear drops pouring down
every ounce of the voice picks up
shattered billion hearts fide into sorrows
The fear of growth terrifies the fact
shivers shimmers through the body
let out a loud voice as it began
plastered petals bloom in the era
may the Autumn bless the spring
Darkens the ocean of a bliss
soul shines through the machine.
Bounces the way we taught themselves
everyday sun burns the sand
It depicts the depth of our world
our thoughts had been drowning
Rapids of the monster we created
they evolve as they reach the mankind
We evolve as we reach the sky
-Magixie

Chapter50

Eyes wandered in the pretty blooms
may the sky born in your dark orbs
flashed the luminosity to look at
Tragically timid to destroy me
Endangered my chaotic life
messier still prettier than cosmos
virgoriously enchanted by those blooms
sculpted me in an Entangled dust
I could die in the orbs that universe beholds...
- Magixie

Chapter51

Traces of you are indeed
parts of you are Lost in mind
as if the still is a fading Glory
memories can breathe in dust
the voice chanting in my head
It felt as if it's never here
you carved me in a magical way
sculpted me that was never before
please hold onto me...
- Magixie

Chapter52

Provoking the beauty
tides of wisdom
piles up the desire
way back to the throne
that grudges the crown
Just a wishker away
shadows taunting you
As you hunt them
Never been in here before ... -
- Magixie

Chapter53

The broken soul snivelled
until it crumbled with madness
shattered glitters murmured goodbye
even hope couldn't help further
will this be the end?
Atleast spare my broken wings
The bitter sweet memories of you
became the forbidden sparkle
I couldn't take the fear
I'm afraid of the care
- Magixie

Chapter54

As the time pass by
the murmurs of your sorrows
I found my comfort engulfed in them
it's the misery that lead me into life
proclaiming the darkness of my depths
blood has been fond by the plum
I'm devastated by the hell
I know I'm a monster
realising I'm much more than chaos
then the fiction steps in
i'm drawn by the perfect fairy takes
making me drown in them
-Magixie

Chapter55

As the rays hit me
I felt the warmth in your love
Tackle down all the problems
miracles wander in the blooms
unseen by the Spirit of shadows
don't let go by the smile
mischeif bounded by the golden lights
sensed all of my beliefs
beauty of the woods in daylight
filled my hollow darkness
may the sun shine through you...
-Magixie

Chapter56

Until the dawn I wishpered
it's the moonlight that spot me
until the fall rise I searched
it's this sunlight that heard me
too pretty to care in my eyes
too cozy to stare in your thoughts
may be it's the way you look
may be it's the way i love
as this lasts for an eternal...
- Magixie

Chapter57

Charms equipped with the momento
Ignite the force with sun
restoring the call of moon
radiating the shine of stars
mixture of heaven squeals in your soul
dark night's remind me of blood moon
you built a perfect chaos in me
-Magixie

Chapter58

Terror is all that grieves
horrified by everything
the only way is hope
when you know what's about to
all the anxious thoughts fill in
let the nervousness wash away
fear petrifies all my emotions
heal your soul which finds peace
- Magixie

Chapter59

It all started with an end
I thought there would be no story
It was all it has been never knew
It was a pretty disaster ever imagined
If it were for you to align
I would kill every star in my galaxy
If It was meant for you
I would still be there in my shattered pieces
you made my hope a waking dream
you made my hope drown in fear
you are still loved by me
-Magixie

Chapter60

Lived by the shadows
picturing it a safe place
locked by the lies
measuring it a hope
masked by the emotions
wandering it's magnificent
thriving by the grief
holding the giggles
The moment I coerced
my mind found its peace
-Magixie

Chapter61

I have been lying to myself
destruction is building itself
chaos are the chores of my mind
melting the disturbed heart
Hell seems good as heaven
Hope is coercing me as always
eerie was a pretty mess
it was supposed to be painful
yet it makes me happy...
-Magixie

Chapter62

Pretty blooms in spring
makes my day with snow
as they would last never
autumn makes them fade
as I cry over the fallen mess
summer brings me myself
As the seasons never let me fail...
-Magixie

Chapter63

I learned to wait
I lost hope in faith
I learned to forget
I realised to forgive
I made myself strong
still you made me weak
~An extract from Magixie's Journel
- Magixie

Chapter64

Wandering in lost world
the sky is set on fire
when everything goes vain
I found myself there
in the corner of flames
Igniting my buried fears
Trauma haunting me
repeating that I belong there
Everything becomes apocalypse
-Magixie

Chapter65

You made me cry in silence
breaking the force of resilience
you blew the catastrophic winds
bleeding the soul that loves
you graze my darkness in light
throwing tantrums in the fight
you were then potential to my hope
making me drown in the weep
you don't let me hate
as if you were my mate.
- Magixie

www.ingramcontent.com/pod-product-compliance
Lightning Source LLC
LaVergne TN
LVHW041232150826
845673LV00008B/2366

* 9 7 9 8 8 9 6 3 2 6 3 4 2 *